Keiko the Whale

The Star of Free Willy®

by William John Ripple

William John Ripple, PhD, works as a university professor and lives in Corvallis, Oregon. His studies include topics in wildlife, ecology, and forestry. He has published three other books on natural resources and numerous articles on subjects relating to wildlife and ecology. Bill's photos appear on pages 30 and 32 (this is page 2).

Paul VanDevelder is an award-winning freelance author and photographer based in Corvallis, Oregon. He has spent the past sixteen years working in the national and international press corps, with daily newspapers, wire services and magazines. Paul's photos appear on pages 10, 20, 24, 26, and 28.

Tim Jewett is a freelance photographer from Portland, Oregon and has 25 years of professional experience. He has won numerous awards for his photographs and has had his work published in Time, Life, Newsweek, People, and other magazines. Tim's photos appear on pages 6, 8, 12, 14, 16, 18, 22, and 37.

Publishing editors Sandy Wadman and Ted Wadman.

Book design and illustration by Larry Clarkberg.

The author thanks Ellen Deehan Clark for editorial comments as well as Keith Swindle and Joe and Gloria Harrod for suggestions and encouragement.

Free Willy is a trademark of Warner Brothers, Inc.

Text copyright © 1998 by William John Ripple. All rights reserved. No part of this publication may be reproduced in any form or by any electronic or mechanical means, including information storage and retrieval systems, without permission in writing from the publisher.

Photograph on page 3 copyright John Greim and Weststock, Inc. Photograph on page 4 copyright Larry Hobbs and Weststock, Inc.

Printed in the United States of America

Publisher's cataloging-in-publication data (provided by Quality Books, Inc.):

Ripple, William J.

    Keiko the whale : the star of Free Willy / by William John Ripple. -- 1st ed.

    p. cm.

    SUMMARY: The true story of the captive orca who starred in the movie Free Willy before being rehabilitated for release into the North Atlantic Ocean.

    Preassigned Library of Congress Catalog Card Number: 98-67216

    ISBN 0-9665844-0-6

    1. Keiko (Whale)--Juvenile literature. 2. Killer whale--Biography--Juvenile literature. 3. Free Willy (Motion Picture)--Miscellanea. 4. Wildlife rehabilitation--Juvenile literature. I. Title.

    QL795.W5R56 1998   599.53'6'0929
                        QBI98-953

Published by:

Nu, Inc.
965 N.W. Wildrose Drive
Corvallis, OR 97330

For Christopher, Jeremy, Lindzie, and NatalieKai and all children whose love for Keiko helps raise awareness of and respect for all whales in oceans around the world.

Orcas are one of the most amazing creatures on earth. They live peaceful lives with their family pods swimming together and hunting for food throughout the oceans of the world.

This is the story about one special Orca named Keiko who was born many years ago off the coast of Iceland in the north Atlantic Ocean. When he was only a two-year-old infant, Keiko was trapped in a fishing net and removed from his family.

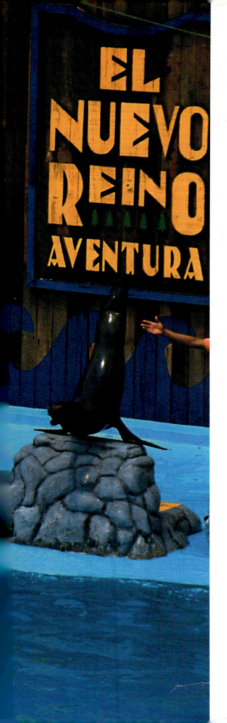

Keiko was sold to entertain people in amusement parks. He was originally moved to Canada, and then eventually he was moved to an amusement park in Mexico City. There he met Karla and Renata who trained him to perform amazing tricks in front of large groups of people.

Keiko quickly became famous for his shows, and he seemed to be loved by everyone especially his trainers and small children. People came from all over Mexico to see him perform. Keiko let Renata ride on his belly as he swam on his back around the pool.

One day, Keiko became the star of the popular movie "Free Willy" where a 12-year-old boy, Jesse, helps free an Orca named "Willy" from a small pool at an amusement park. Unlike in the movie, the real Keiko remained at the amusement park after the filming of the movie. Keiko was still without his family and was becoming ill in his small pool in Mexico where the water was too warm for him.

When word spread that Keiko was still in Mexico, a rescue plan was started by those who were concerned about this magnificent whale. School children and adults worked together to raise money to build Keiko a new home. Work started on building a new pool for Keiko at an aquarium in Oregon. The project was a race against time since Keiko was becoming more ill.

Finally, Keiko's new home was ready for him. Just before he was moved to Oregon, many people from all over Mexico came to watch him deliver an outstanding last performance in Mexico City.

Nearly everyone in Mexico was sad to see Keiko go since they were losing a friend that they loved very much, but they knew the move would be best for Keiko.

Keiko was gently placed into a large container that was filled with ice to keep him cool. His trainers put lotion on him to keep his skin moist during the long trip out of water. Keiko rode in a cargo plane which landed in Newport, Oregon 18 hours after leaving Mexico City. Keiko seemed to be very patient during the long trip, but he needed to be placed in cold water soon.

Finally, Keiko was fitted with a sling, lifted by a crane from his container, and gently lowered into his deep new pool which was filled with clean, cool Pacific Ocean water. Keiko was very excited when he swam in his new pool which was much larger and colder than his pool in Mexico City.

Keiko was welcomed to his new home by many children, some who helped in his rescue by raising part of the money to build his new pool. The children of Newport were happy to have Keiko come to live with them, but they knew it was only a temporary home and that his journey would not end until he was back in the Atlantic Ocean with his original family.

Both Karla and Renata came up to Oregon with Keiko to be with him and show his new trainers how they took care of this whale whom they loved so very much. Karla liked to use a whistle and hand signals to train Keiko.

When they were sure that Keiko was doing well in his new home, both Karla and Renata sadly left Keiko and returned to their home in Mexico.

Keiko does not perform tricks in his new pool at the Oregon Coast Aquarium, but he does delight visitors by swimming in front of large windows where thousands of people watch him every day.

Keiko works and plays with his new skilled trainers to improve his strength and general health in order to prepare him for living in the open sea again.

Keiko eats 165 pounds of fish per day. His trainers have placed live fish in his pool in order to teach him to hunt and eat live swimming fish. These hunting skills will be necessary for Keiko to be able to survive in the wild North Atlantic Ocean.

→ Notice that Keiko is missing a tooth on his right side. The tooth was broken, so it was removed by a doctor. This missing tooth will not cause Keiko any problems with eating.

Keiko rolls over on his back so his care givers can draw samples of blood to check on his health. Everyone wants to make sure Keiko is completely healthy before he is released to live with other Orcas back at sea.

When Keiko first arrived in Oregon, he had a major skin rash and was underweight for an Orca of his age.

Keiko has gained nearly a ton while living at the Oregon Coast Aquarium and his skin rash has completely disappeared. Keiko has become much stronger and more active than when he lived in his small warm pool in Mexico.

It will be both a happy and sad time when the day comes for Keiko to return to his family at sea. We will be sad to see him go and will dearly miss this gentle whale. At the same time, we can celebrate that Keiko will be free once again:

Free to swim and play in the deep blue sea.

Free to sing the songs of an Orca whale.

Free to be on his final journey home.

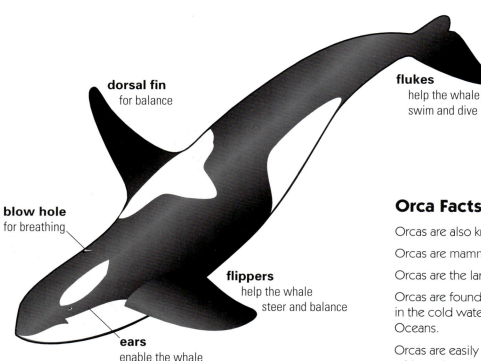

dorsal fin for balance

flukes help the whale swim and dive

blow hole for breathing

flippers help the whale steer and balance

ears enable the whale to hear over 20 miles (32 km)

whale food

Orca Facts

Orcas are also known as Killer Whales.

Orcas are mammals and breath air with their lungs.

Orcas are the largest members of the dolphin family.

Orcas are found in all oceans of the world especially in the cold waters of the Arctic and Antarctic Oceans.

Orcas are easily identified by their striking black and white color patterns.

Orcas live with their families in pods and stay together for life.

It is unknown how long Orcas live, but some people think they can live as long as 50 to 80 years.

Female Orcas are much smaller than male Orcas. Adult females can weigh as much as 4 tons and be over 20 feet long, while adult males can weigh over 8 tons and exceed 30 feet in length.

Orcas are not protected in some parts of the world and are still being captured, removed from their families, and sold to amusement parks.

Keiko Facts

1977 or **1978** Keiko was born in the Atlantic Ocean near Iceland.

1979 Keiko was captured and taken to Iceland.

1982 Keiko was moved to Marineland in Ontario, Canada.

1985 Keiko was sold to Reino Aventura, an amusement park in Mexico City for $350,000.

1992 Keiko was filmed as the star Orca in the movie "Free Willy" where the whale played by Keiko was helped to freedom by a young boy.

1993 The Free Willy-Keiko foundation was formed to rehabilitate and possibly release Keiko back to the wild.

1995 A new large pool was built for Keiko in Newport, Oregon.

1996 Keiko arrived at his new pool at the Oregon Coast Aquarium.

1997 Keiko's health and weight improved. His weight increased to 9620 pounds, an increase of 1900 pounds since moving to Oregon.

1998 Keiko started catching and eating live fish and he continues his training for his release into a sea pen in the North Atlantic.

Keiko's Journey